Windows 10 For Beginners:

Simple Step-by-Step Manual on How To Customize Windows 10 For Your Needs

Disclamer: All photos used in this book, including the cover photo were made available under a Attribution-NonCommercial-ShareAlike 2.0 Generic

Table of content

Introduction 5

Chapter 1 – Getting started with windows 10 6

A new beginning 6

One step back and two steps forward 7

Prepare your computer for Windows 10 7

Can your PC run it? 7

Free up space 8

Save your information to the cloud or an outer drive 8

Make an image backup 8

Chapter 2 – Upgradation and clean installation of Windows 10 10

Make beyond any doubt your PC is qualified for Windows 10 10

Back up your PC 10

Update your present Windows adaptation 10

Sit tight for the Windows 10 prompt 11

Chapter 3 – Start using Windows 10 13

Marking into Windows 10 13

Exploring the desktop 14

Opening applications 15

Looking for records and applications 17

Changing your settings 18

Opening the Settings application 19

Shutting down your PC 20

Tips for managing multiple windows 21

Demonstrating the desktop 22

Customizing your desktop 22

Change the text dimension..23

Change ClearType settings 25

Chapter 4 – Get more familiar with Windows 10...27

Simplify the Start menu 27

Cover up Cortana 28

Utilize the Control Panel rather than the Settings application......................................28

Use of Microsoft edge 29

Managing your account 29

Marking out and exchanging users 31

Managing user accounts 31

Setting parental controls 32

Chapter 5 – Getting your Windows 10 secured..35

User Account Control 35

Windows Defender 35

Windows Firewall..35

Windows SmartScreen...35

Chapter 6 – Additional features of Windows 10 37

Start inking...37

Delete line-by-line 38

New photo app in windows 10 38

Add folder..39

Alter and upgrade 39

Conclusion 41

Introduction

Microsoft has released the first specialized sneak peak of its new Windows 10 working plan. With the new OS, the organization would like to handle the feedback it confronted with Windows 8, which was improved for a touch UI, giving a mediocre user experience to the desktop and portable workstation users.

Senior vice president of Microsoft Terry Myerson composed on the Windows blog that this new Windows must be developed starting from the earliest stage of being portable in the first place. This new Windows must offer their users some assistance with being profitable in both their computerized work and their advanced life. That new Windows are none other than Windows 10.

They planned Windows 10 to convey a more individualized computing knowledge over a large number of gadgets. It is an affair which has been enhanced for every type of gadget and it is the commonplace for all the users.

It will likewise control the general surroundings of the company, center to gadgets making up the pool of Things, and everything from lifts to ATMs to heart rate screens to wearables etc. Regardless of which Windows 10 gadget the users utilize, the experience will feel good, and there will be a solitary, general Windows Store where they can discover, attempt and purchase Universal Windows apps without facing any sort of problem in any case.

Chapter 1 – Getting started with windows 10

This new Windows is accessible as a free overhaul for existing Windows 7 and Windows 8's non-corporate users. It is developed starting from the earliest stage after Microsoft's vision of a bounded together operating system that compasses all gadgets without distancing any of the stages. It's an endeavor to shield Microsoft's disintegrating programming dominion, assaulted on all sides by Google and Apple.

A new beginning

The Start menu is back, it's verging on interesting how calming that is. That modest Start button has been an installation on the lower left corner of the Windows desktop since the halcyon days of Windows 95, offering rapid access to applications and settings.

The past sits on the left which is a flawless section with alternate ways to your most utilized applications. Press the "All Apps" button and you'll get a sequential rundown of all the applications. There are envelopes in there as well, you are just required to press them, and additional options will fly out, much the same as they generally have.

There are beautiful, vivified live tiles that appeared in Windows 8, pulling twofold obligation as alternate routes to application and educational gadgets. You can resize these live tiles, dragging them will go to mastermind them into gatherings and pin the same number of applications as you'd like, then the whole Start menu can be contracted or extended to suit your loving. It's basically a scaled down form of the full screen Start menu you found in Windows 8. At that point unpin them to extract them from your PC, abandoning you with the tight section of as often as possible utilized applications which you have known for so long.

One step back and two steps forward

The Start menu in Windows 10 is affirmation that Windows 8 possibly have been a bit too ground breaking. But, Microsoft hasn't relinquished that vision of bringing together all way of gadgets under a solitary working plan.

To begin, there's no gap between the Windows 8-style of Cutting edge applications, you get from the Windows application store, and those you introduce the way it was done in the good old days. Everything exists as a conventional windowed application, sharing space on the desktop. In case you're on a two-in-one gadget like Microsoft's Surface Pro 3, click the console off and Windows 10 will change to tablet mode. The Start menu and your applications will extend to take up the whole screen, and the greater part of the random applications and alternate routes on your taskbar will vanish, to give your finger less snags to hit.

Prepare your computer for Windows 10

Notwithstanding an enhanced outline and better usefulness, Windows 10 denote the arrival of a genuine Start button. Before you bounce right in and get introduced to Windows 10, you ought to take a couple of minutes and set up your PC to guarantee the overhaul procedure that goes off effortlessly. Here I will give you information which will guide you through the progressions of checking for overhauls, moving down your own data and making an immeasurably critical plan picture.

Can your PC run it?

You can verify whether your machine is fit for running Windows 10 right from your desktop or not. You will require a PC or tablet running Windows 7 Service Pack 1 or Windows 8.1 Update. From the desktop, click on the little Windows symbol situated at the right end of the taskbar, and select the "Check my PC" option from the left menu.

Free up space

You will require no less than 16GB of free space to introduce Windows 10. To check the amount of free space is on your hard drive, go to Computer, right-tap the C:/drive, and select Properties. You can free up some space by tapping the Disk Cleanup button. This normally won't free up enough space, so you might likewise need to uninstall programs that you no more utilize.

To uninstall a Windows 8 project, go to the Start menu (the screen with the tiles), right-tap the tile you need to install, and select Uninstall. You can likewise uninstall programs through the Control Panel, which you can scan for in Windows 8. In Windows 7, tap the Start button, trailed by the Control Panel, and select Uninstall a program.

Save your information to the cloud or an outer drive

In any case if you are moving up to Windows 10 or not, it's generally a smart thought to save your information. You can utilize a cloud administration, for example, OneDrive, Dropbox or Google Drive, or an outside hard drive. Windows 8 users can likewise utilize the File History highlight to naturally move down individual documents.

Make an image backup

Both Windows 7 and Windows 8.1 accompany an instrument that gives you a chance to make an image file which is a full reinforcement of everything on your PC. Head to the Control Panel and select Move down your PC under the Systems and Security area.

Toward the end of the procedure, you will have the option to make a plan repair disk. This can be utilized to offer you some assistance with repairing Windows if you keep running into any issues. You can likewise make a USB recuperation drive, which you can figure out how to do here.

If you wind up restoring your PC from a plan picture, you can do as such in the Control Panel. Begin by writing recuperation in the inquiry box, click Recovery, trailed by advanced recuperation strategies, and select to utilize the image backup you made before.

Chapter 2 – Upgradation and clean installation of Windows 10

Make beyond any doubt your PC is qualified for Windows 10

Windows 10 is free for anybody running the most recent rendition of Windows 7, Windows 8 and Windows 8.1 on their portable PC, desktop or tablet PC. You can make sense of which form your PC by going to Microsoft's site. You must be a manager on your PC, implying that you possess the PC and set it up yourself. It's conceivable that you won't have the capacity to redesign work PCs that are overseen by an IT division all alone.

Back up your PC

To ensure the majority of the documents you have on your PC, I prescribe that you move down your PC, just if something turns out badly during the redesign process.

Update your present Windows adaptation

You should introduce the greater part of the overhauls for the present form of Windows you have on your machine. If you've set up programmed upgrades, you ought to be good to go, however twofold check first.

- On Windows 7, go to Start, Control Panel, System and Security and Windows Update.

- On Windows 8 and 8.1, go to Start, PC Settings, Update and recuperation, and Windows Update.

- On all forms of Windows, your PC will you if there are any accessible upgrades and walk you through the procedure of downloading and introducing them.

- You may need to check for and introduce overhauls a few times to complete this procedure.

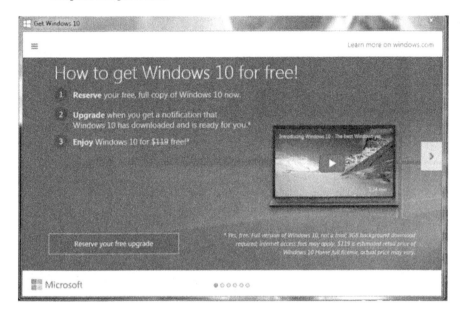

Sit tight for the Windows 10 prompt

Once your PC has the most recent overhauls, you'll have to sit tight for a Windows symbol to appear in the taskbar on your desktop, telling you can hold Windows 10. Take after the bearings on the screen to tell Microsoft that you might want the Windows 10 upgrade. You may enter your email location to affirm the upgrade, however it is a bit much.

When you're done with the reservation purpose, whatever you can do is kick back and sit tight for Microsoft to naturally send Windows 10 to your PC, a procedure that can take a few days or weeks. When it's an ideal opportunity to introduce the upgrade, you will get a warning on your PC.

If you've completed all the above steps and would prefer not to hold up one more moment to get Windows 10, there is an approach to speed things up. But, utilize this procedure at your own particular risk, on the grounds that it can be more confounded than basically sitting tight for the upgrade to arrive.

If you have a Windows 7 or 8 PC, you can introduce Microsoft's new Windows 10 operating system totally for nothing. If you take after this technique, Windows 10 will bring along the greater part of your information, applications and the greater part of your plan settings from your more seasoned operating system and it can unfavorably influence execution.

Chapter 3 – Start using Windows 10

Whether you're utilizing another PC with Windows 10 or a more established machine that was as of late redesigned, this lesson will demonstrate you the nuts and bolts of utilizing this form of Windows.

Marking into Windows 10

You'll likely be requested that make a Microsoft account the very time you utilize Windows 10 if you don't have one as of now. Starting here on, at whatever point you turn on the PC you'll have to sign into that record. To do this, sort your secret password into the case and press Enter.

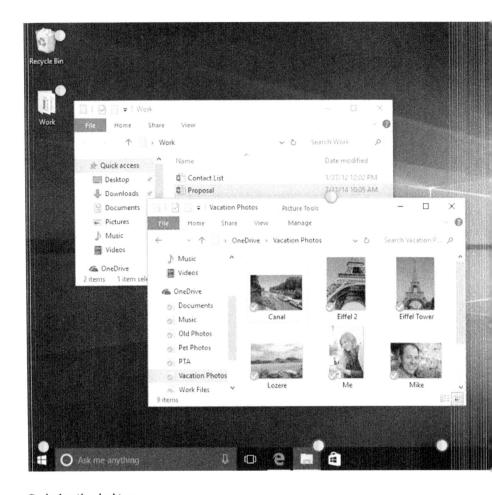

Exploring the desktop

Once you've marked in, the first thing you'll see is the desktop. You can think about the desktop as the principle workspace for your PC. From here, you can see and deal with your documents, open applications, get to the Internet, and a great deal more.

Click the buttons in the intuitive underneath to end up more acquainted with the Windows 10 desktop:

Opening applications

You'll utilize the Start menu to open applications on your PC, much the same as with past variants of Windows. To do this, snap the Start button in the bottom left corner, then pick the fancied application. If you don't see the one you need, select all applications to see a full rundown of uses. In the illustration beneath, we're opening OneNote.

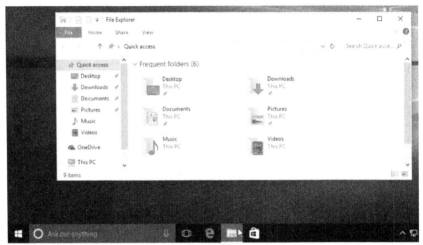

Working with documents

You'll utilize the File Explorer to deal with your documents and envelopes. To open File Explorer, tap the File Explorer symbol on the taskbar or double tap any envelope on your desktop.

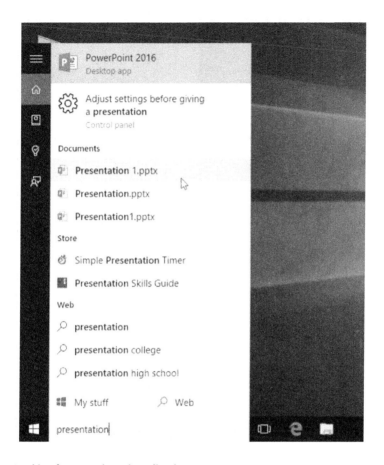

Looking for records and applications

To look for something on your PC, like a specific record or application, tap the Start button, then begin writing. On the other hand, you can press the Windows key on the console to start a pursuit. In the sample underneath, we're scanning for a presentation document.

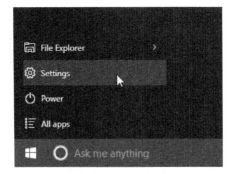

Changing your settings

You'll utilize the Settings application to change the most critical settings on your PC, similar to your system and presentation choices. To open the application, tap the Start menu, then select Settings.

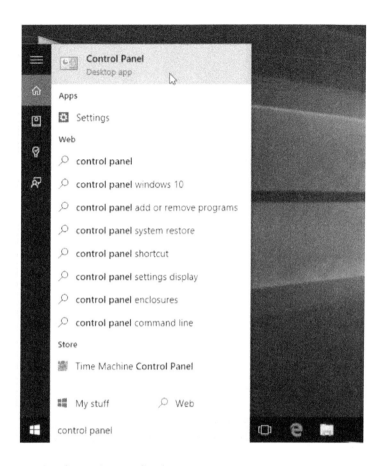

Opening the Settings application

You can likewise utilize the Control Panel to conform your settings, much the same as in prior forms of Windows. On the other hand, there are a few options that must be gotten to from the Settings application, such as including another user. As a result of this, you'll most likely utilize the Settings application all the more regularly.

Shutting down your PC

When you're set utilizing your PC, it's vital to close it down appropriately. To do this, snap the Start button, then pick Power > Shut Down.

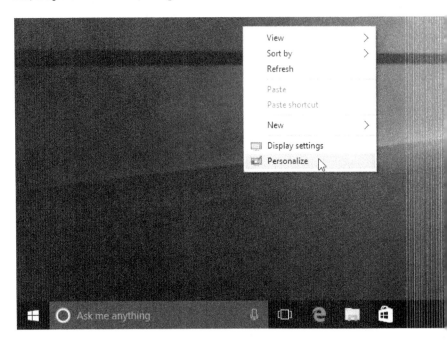

Tips for managing multiple windows

Windows 10 has a few components that make it less demanding to multi-assignment and work with numerous windows in the meantime.

Snap

Snap permits you to resize windows rapidly, which is particularly helpful when you need to see two windows one next to the other. To do this, snap and drag the wanted window to one side or right until the cursor achieves the edge of the screen, then release the mouse. The window will snap into spot. To unsnap a window, essentially snap and drag the window down.

Flip

You can utilize Flip option to switch between open windows. To do this, press and hold the Alt key on your console, then press the Tab key. Keep squeezing the Tab key until the wanted window is chosen.

Task view

The Task window element is like Flip, yet it works a bit differently. To open Task perspective, tap the Task perspective button close to the bottom left corner of the taskbar. Elective, you can squeeze Windows key+Tab on your console. The greater part of your open windows will show up, and you can snap to pick any window you need.

Virtual desktops

Rather than continuing everything open on the same desktop, you can move some of your windows to a virtual desktop to get them off the beaten path. This element wasn't accessible in past variants of Windows, and it's particularly useful for dealing with a considerable measure of windows in the meantime. To make another desktop, open Task view, then select new desktop close to the bottom right corner.

Once you've made numerous desktops, you can utilize Task perspective to switch between them. You can likewise move windows between desktops. To do this, open Task view, then snap and drag a window to the sought desktop. To close a virtual desktop, open Task view and tap the X in the upper-right corner of any desktop you need to close.

Demonstrating the desktop

If you have a considerable measure of windows open in the meantime, it can be difficult to see the desktop. At the point when this happens, you can tap the bottom right corner of the taskbar to minimize every single open window. Simply click it again to restore the minimized windows.

Customizing your desktop

Windows 10 makes it simple to tweak the look and feel of your desktop. To get to the Personalization settings, right-click at any place on the desktop, then select Personalize starting from the drop menu. The Personalization settings will show up.

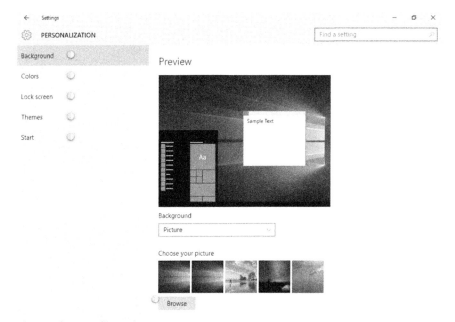

Change the text dimension

If you experience issues seeing the content on your PC, you can build the text dimension. Expanding the text dimension will likewise build the span of symbols and different things on your desktop.

Open the Settings application, then select System.

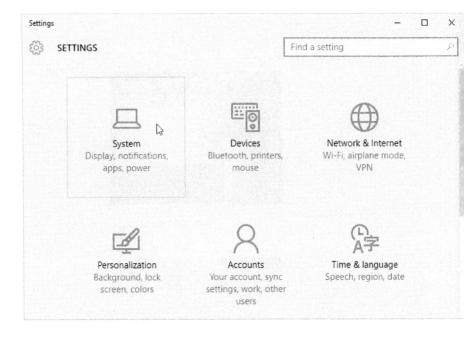

The Display choices will show up. Utilize the slider to choose the coveted thing size. Note that a bigger size may meddle with the way a few things show up on the screen.

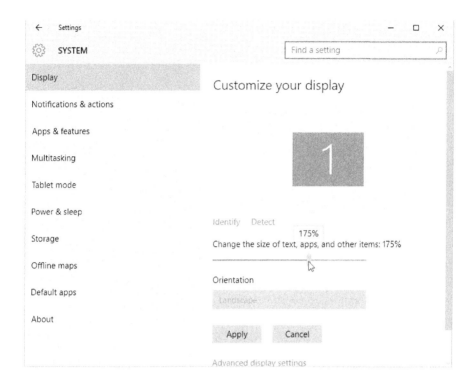

Snap Apply to spare your progressions. You might then need to restart your PC for these progressions to produce results.

Change ClearType settings

ClearType permits you to calibrate how the content on your PC looks, which enhances decipherability. From the Display settings, select advanced settings.

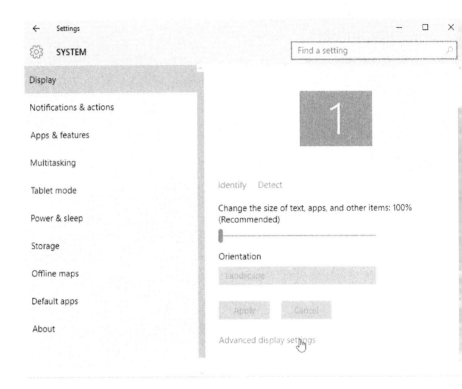

Chapter 4 – Get more familiar with Windows 10

At the point when Windows 8 was released in 2012, numerous users whined that it was confounding and difficult to utilize. Subsequently, Windows 10 looks and feels more like more seasoned renditions. Still, there are a few changes you may discover befuddling or irritating. If you need Windows 10 to feel significantly more like Windows 7 or Windows XP, here are a few tips I can propose.

Simplify the Start menu

Windows 10 utilizes an extended Start menu, which is extensively bigger than past variants. Then again, if you'd like to utilize the customary and more slender Start menu, there is an answer. In the first place, you'll have to unpin the greater part of the applications in the Start menu. To do this, simply right-click a tile, then select Unpin from Start. In this sample, we've as of now unpinned everything aside from the Calendar application.

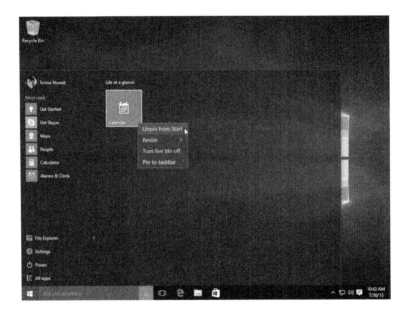

Once you've unpinned the majority of the tiles, float your mouse over the right fringe of the Start menu, then snap and drag it to one side.

Cover up Cortana

One element not accessible in past forms of Windows is Cortana, a virtual right hand that can offer you some assistance with creating updates, discover documents, and that's just the beginning. But, if you'd lean toward not to utilize Cortana or if you simply would prefer not to see the symbol on your taskbar, you can shroud this element. To do this, right-tap the taskbar, then select Cortana > Hidden.

Utilize the Control Panel rather than the Settings application

Dissimilar to past forms of Windows, the majority of your essential settings will be changed through the new Settings application as opposed to the Control Panel. Still, there are numerous settings you can transform from the Control Panel and those that can't will divert you to the Settings application when essential. To open the Control Panel, press the Windows key on your console, sort Control Panel, and then press finish.

Use of Microsoft edge

Another enormous change in Windows 10 is Microsoft Edge, the new default web program. As a rule, Microsoft Edge is more secure than Internet Explorer, and it ought to likewise be speedier and better with the cutting edge Web. In any case, if you like to utilize internet explorer more often than not you can reset it as your default web program.

- Open the Settings application, then select System.

- Explore to the Default apps options.

- Select Web program, then pick Internet Explorer. IE will be set as your default program.

Managing your account

A user account permits you to sign into Windows 10. As a matter of course, your PC as of now has one user account, which you were required to make when setting up Windows interestingly. Yet, if you plan to share your PC, you can make a different user account for every individual from your home or office.

Joining users to a Microsoft account will offer them some assistance with getting the most out of Windows. In any case, if a user inclines toward not to make a Microsoft account, you can likewise include a nearby user account that exists just on your PC.

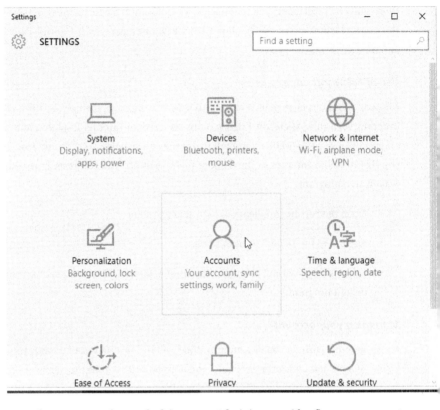

Note that you must be marked in as an Administrator (the first user account made on your PC) to include another user.

- To include another user (with a Microsoft account):

- Open the Settings application, then select Accounts.

- Select Family and different users. Look down to the Other Users area, then pick Add another person to this PC.

- If the new user as of now has a Microsoft account, enter the related email address, then snap Next.

- The user can then sign into the PC with his or her Microsoft account data. Note that it may take a few minutes to design a user's settings when signing in with a Microsoft account surprisingly.

To include another nearby user (without a Microsoft account):

- From the Account settings, snap Add another person to this PC.

- Select the individual I need to include doesn't have an email address.

- The account creation screen will show up. Select add a user without a Microsoft account.

- Enter an account name, then sort the fancied secret word. It's essential to pick an in number secret key—at the end of the day, one that is anything but difficult to recollect yet difficult for others to figure.

- The nearby user can then sign into the PC with this account data.

Marking out and exchanging users

If you're finished utilizing your account, you can sign out. To do this, click the Start button, select the present account in the upper left corner, then pick Sign out. Different users will then have the capacity to sign in from the lock screen.

It's additionally simple to switch between users without marking out or shutting your current apps. Exchanging users will bolt the present user, so you won't have to stress over another person getting to your account. To do this, select the present account, then pick the coveted user starting from the drop menu. You can utilize this same strategy to change back to the next user.

Managing user accounts

As a matter of course, the user account you made when setting up your PC is an Administrator account. An Administrator account permits you to roll out top-level improvements to the PC, such as including new users or modifying specific settings. Any users you add are consequently doled out to a Standard user account, which ought to meet the regular needs of most users. You will most likely just need one Administrator account on a common PC, however you have the option to elevate any user to an Administrator account if you need.

From the Family and different users options, select the coveted user, then snap Change account sort.

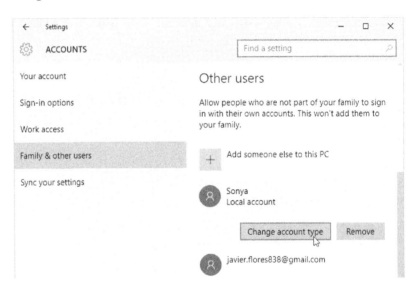

Select the coveted choice starting from the drop list, then snap OK. In this case, we'll pick Administrator.

The user will now have authoritative benefits.

Setting parental controls

Windows offers an assortment of parental controls that can offer you some assistance with monitoring your actions of youngsters and shield them from unseemly substance. For instance, you can confine certain apps and sites or point of confinement the measure of time a user can spend on the PC. You'll have to include a family account for every user you need to screen. Every user will likewise need a Microsoft account; you can't empower parental controls on a nearby account.

- From the Family and different options for users, select add a relative.

- Select Add a youngster, enter the new user's email address, then click next.

- The new part will then need to affirm the expansion to your family assemble from his or her inbox.

- When this is done, select manage family settings on the web.

- A page will open in another program window. From here, select the craved user to set parental controls.

Click the buttons in the intelligent underneath to take in more about setting parental controls:

| Microsoft | Account | Search Microsoft.com | Support |

Home | Your info | Services & subscriptions | Payment & billing | Devices | **Family** | Security & privacy

Recent activity

Merced Flores
flores.merced@yahoo.com

July 25 through today

Activity reporting   **Email weekly reports to me**
⬤ On   ⬤ On

Recent activity
Web browsing
Apps & games
Screen time

Web browsing   Settings

When your child browses websites they'll appear here.

34

Chapter 5 – Getting your Windows 10 secured

Windows 10 incorporates various inherent components to keep your PC safe from infections, malware, and that's only the tip of the iceberg. You can take in more about the absolute most essential components underneath.

User Account Control

User Account Control cautions you when a system or user endeavors to change your PC's settings. Your screen will be incidentally bolted until an Administrator can affirm the progressions. This ensures your PC against pernicious programming and accidental changes. User Account Control additionally permits you to choose how regularly you'll get these notices.

Windows Defender

Windows Defender gives antivirus and malware assurance to your PC. Notwithstanding examining your PC for conceivably destructive applications, Windows Defender gives constant insurance, twofold checking every document or application you open without backing off your PC.

Windows Firewall

Of course, Windows will ensure your Internet association with Windows Firewall. A firewall keeps unapproved access from outside associations and shields your system from risks that could hurt your PC.

Windows SmartScreen

At whatever point your PC recognizes a security risk from a record or application, Windows SmartScreen will notify you with a full-screen cautioning. At whatever point you see this notice screen, you ought to pick not to open the record or application unless you can verify that it won't harm your PC.

Chapter 6 – Additional features of Windows 10

Windows 10's cutting edge program, Microsoft Edge, has a few new elements you'll need to investigate, including a diversion free perusing perspective and a quick, secure rendering motor.

In any case, the coolest new element is inking - the capacity to draw, compose on, and for the most part stamp up Web pages from specifically inside of the program. You can share your stamped up manifestations by means of email or through informal organizations, or you can spare them to OneNote.

Start inking

When you see a Web page you need to "ink," tap the little symbol that resembles a pen and paper in the upper right corner of the program window. There are just around five symbols absolute, so this shouldn't be excessively difficult, making it impossible to discover.

To utilize a highlighter, which will give you a chance to highlight content and pictures as opposed to drawing over them, tap the highlighter button. Click the highlighter button a second time to choose your highlighter shading and shape with six colors and three shapes.

If you incline toward writing to composing or drawing, you can utilize the content apparatus to make remarks on the page. To do this, snap the content device button and afterward click anyplace on the page. A numbered pin will show up at that spot, and beside it you'll see a content box, in which you can sort whatever you need.

If you need to clean up the page, you can close the content box by tapping on the numbered pin. The pin will remain where it is, however the content box will minimize. To revive the content box, essentially tap the pin once more. You can likewise move the content box by clicking and dragging the numbered pin.

To erase both the remark pin and the content box, tap the rubbish can symbol in the lower right corner of the content box. One thing to note when you're utilizing the content instrument is that all "ink" imprints will show up over all content boxes.

The cut-out apparatus will likewise transform your cursor into a cross-hair, so you can clasp out a segment of the page. It works like the Snipping Tool - click the cut-out apparatus symbol, and the page will become dim until you select a segment of it. When you have a segment chosen, you'll see a little duplicate symbol in the lower right corner; click this to duplicate your clasp (you can glue it into another system, for example, Microsoft Paint, if you need to spare it).

Delete line-by-line

To delete the whole page, tap the eraser device button a second time and a menu will appear with one option, clear all ink.

New photo app in windows 10

Windows 10 has another Photos application that accomplishes more than simply show your photos as a slideshow. This new default application sorts out your photos by date taken and even makes curated collections for you, includes a couple of pleasant altering devices for picture upgrade, and gives you a chance to share pictures by means of informal communities and email. While it's not going to supplant Photoshop at any point in the near future, the Photos application is justified regardless of a look.

The new photographs application has two principle areas: Collection and Albums. In the Collection segment, you'll see a gathering of every one of your photographs, assembled by date taken backward sequential request. If you need to rapidly discover photographs from a sure time period without looking through the majority of the photographs in your gathering, snap or tap out on the town to zoom out to a rundown of every single past month.

Add folder

At in the first place, the main photographs in your Photos application will be those from your Pictures envelope and perhaps anything saved money on your OneDrive. To add another envelope to the Photos application, open the application, go to Settings and under the Sources area, snap or tap add an organizer. Discover the organizer you need to include, select it, and click Add this envelope to Pictures.

If you'd rather not have your OneDrive photographs appear in the Photos application, go to Settings and turn off Show my photographs and recordings from OneDrive.

Alter and upgrade

The new Photos application has some altering elements, including channels and a single tick Enhance button that applies some fundamental fixes.

To alter a photograph in the Photos application, click on the photograph to open it and snap the pencil symbol to open the altering stage. To one side of your photograph, you'll see the different classifications: Basic fixes, channels, light, shading, and impacts. Fundamental fixes incorporate a single tick Enhance button, and also turn, trimming, fixing, red-eye, and correct, which gives you a chance to tap and smooth away flaws.

In the Light menu, you can conform brilliance, difference, highlights, and shadows. Shine and complexity are really clear as crystal, however the highlight and shadow agents are valuable for settling a photographs that has different lighting levels e.g., splendid recognizes that should be diminished or extremely dull detects that should be lit up. In the Color menu, you can change temperature, tint, and immersion; there's additionally an element called Color support, which gives you a chance to choose one shading and make it pretty much unmistakable.

The Filters and Effects menu are the place you can get your Instagram-style settle: The Filters menu offers six channels, including highly contrasting, while the Effects menu gives you a chance to include a vignette impact, blur the sides of the picture to dark or white, or tilt-shift the core interest.

While you're altering your picture, you can contrast it and the first by clicking and holding the think about button at the highest point of the screen. The top menu has fix/re-try buttons, and additionally the choices to spare the first picture or spare a duplicate of the picture.

Conclusion

Microsoft is gaining solid ground with Windows 10, and they are on track to make it accessible to all of the people. Also, in light of the fact that they have constructed Windows 10 to be conveyed as administration, this point of reference is only the start of the new era of Windows. Starting after that, users can expect continuous development and security upgrades for their Windows 10 gadgets, including more propelled security and administration capacities for organizations.

Users will keep on offering them with some assistance with creating Windows 10 even after this current summer's introductory release, because of the 3.9 million and developing Windows Insiders who are offering us some assistance with building and test Windows 10. Microsoft is thankful for this significant input that is offering them some assistance with offering the best Windows ever, for organizations and buyers, over all gadgets. You, as well, can join the Windows Insider Program today and start discovering Windows 10.

CPSIA information can be obtained
at www.ICGtesting.com
Printed in the USA
LVOW04s1827131016

508652LV00022B/672/P